# My First Book of Tagalog Words

Published in 2006 by Tuttle Publishing, an imprint of Periplus Editions (HK) Ltd.

**www.tuttlepublishing.com**

ISBN 978-0-8048-5014-8
*(Originally published with ISBN 978-0-8048-3819-1; LCC No. 2006905343)*

**Distributors**

**North America, Latin America and Europe**
Tuttle Publishing
364 Innovation Drive
North Clarendon,
VT 05759-9436 USA
Tel: 1(802) 773 8930
Fax: 1 (802) 773 6993
info@tuttlepublishing.com
www.tuttlepublishing.com

**Japan**
Tuttle Publishing
Yaekari Building 3F,
5-4-12 Osaki Shinagawa-Ku,
Tokyo 141-0032
Tel: (81) 3 5437 0171
Fax: (81) 3 5437 0755
sales@tuttle.co.jp
www.tuttle.co.jp

**Asia Pacific**
Berkeley Books Pte Ltd.
3 Kallang Sector #04-01,
Singapore 349278
Tel: (65) 6741 2178
Fax (65) 6741 2179
inquiries@periplus.com.sg
www.tuttlepublishing.com

Printed in Malaysia

26  25  24  23  22      9  8  7  6      2206TO

# My First Book of Tagalog Words

## An ABC Rhyming Book of Filipino Language and Culture

by Liana Romulo
Illustrated by Jaime Laurel

**TUTTLE** Publishing

Tokyo | Rutland, Vermont | Singapore

**Author's Preface**

The words in this book are probably already familiar to children in Philippine households all over the world, as they are frequently used in everyday language. In choosing these specific words, my intention was to teach preschoolers (with English as a first language) what the words mean and how they're spelled, through illustration and memory-enhancing rhyme. After having *My First Book of Tagalog Words* read to them a few times, children will come away with a more precise understanding of vocabulary they might have already picked up at home.

Family appellations, such as *anak*[1] and *lola*,[2] are easily grasped, as they are most common and registered by children at the heart level. Colloquial expressions, such as *naku*[3] and *ewan*,[4] which are difficult to translate, are finally demystified when accompanied by pictures. References to dishes, like *pansit*[5] and *champorado*,[6] inject a bit of Philippine life and culture into the wordplay. Names of Philippine figures and sites, such as Quezon[7] and Vigan,[8] impart a sense of history. Other words, like *hati*[9] and *galing*,[10] have multiple forms and meanings. In the interest of keeping things simple in this first book of a series, I have chosen to define these words only one way: as the word is most likely to be used among children.

The Philippine alphabet does not include the letters C, F, X, Z, Q, V, and J; however, a great number of words using these letters have been adopted into everyday language from Spanish and American colonizers. These are words, such as *zipper* and *jeepney*. Filipino is the national language of the Philippines, and a standardized dialect of Tagalog.

*anak*[1] child or offspring

*lola*[2] grandmother

*naku*[3] *Naku* is used to express distress, and is similar to the interjection "Oh no!"

*ewan*[4] *Ewanko* is a slang expression that means "I don't know."

*pansit*[5] noodles

*champorado*[6] hot porridge made with rice and chocolate, sometimes eaten with dried fish

Quezon[7] Manuel L. Quezon was born in 1878. He served as president of the Philippines from 1935 until his death in 1944.

Vigan[8] Vigan is a historic town in northern Philippines. It was named a World Heritage site in 1999.

*hati*[9] In its verb form *hati* means to divide something in half; for example, food. As an adjective it means "halved" or "divided." As a noun it might refer to the part in one's hair.

*galing*[10] *Galing*, as it is used in this book, refers to the boy's excellent performance. As a noun *galing* means "source" or "origin." In its verb form it means to "recuperate from illness."

**A** is for *anak*,
which isn't my name,
but that's what Mama calls me.
To say **"my child"**
would be sort of the same.

5

**B** is for *butiki*,
a house **lizard**. That's all.
It climbs on the ceiling,
from where it could fall!

6

**C** is for *champorado*,
**chocolate-and-rice porridge**,
believe it or not.
I have it for breakfast.
It's best when it's hot.

7

**D** is for *dahon*,
**leaves** rustling coolly in the heat
on trees in our garden, next to
mangoes heavy and sweet.

**E** is for *ewan*.
That's what we say
when we **don't know** the answer
by the end of the day.

9

**F** is for *Filipino*.
That's what I am.
I was **born in the Philippines**.
That's me ... in the pram!

**G** is for *galing*,
always so nice to hear!
A word of **praise** or approval,
it brings me good cheer.

**H** is for *hati*,
a word Mama uses at meals,
because it means to **share half**
with my sister who squeals.

**I** is for *ibon*,
a **bird** in the sky high up above,
a cute little duckling,
or maybe a dove.

**J** is for **jeepneys**,
miniature **buses** plying the street.
They're noisy and colorful.
I think they're neat!

**K** is for *kumot*,
my favorite **blanket**,
warm in my bed.
And then there's the pillow
to cradle my head.

L is for *Lola*,
who loves me most of all.
She's my **grandmother**.
She comforts me when I fall.

**M** is for *medyas*,
pulled snugly over my toes.
I have green ones and white ones
and a pair with rainbows.

**N** is for *naku*!
Just like **"oh no!"** you'd exclaim
if you broke something precious
or lost in a game.

**O** is for *ospital*,
where my **sister was born**,
and I brought her a toy:
a bright yellow unicorn!

**P** is for *pansit*.
Oh, **noodles**, my favorite dish.
It's nice with pork, beef, or chicken.
But, please, not with fish!

**Q** is for **Quezon**,
**president during the Second World War**.
Overlooking Quezon City
is a monument to him, therefore.

**R** is for *relo*,
a **timepiece** of any kind,
so we're always on schedule
and never run behind.

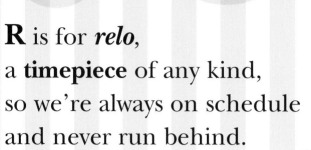
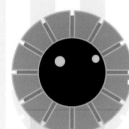

**S** is for *salamat*.
That's what we say
when we are **grateful**.
It's the polite way.

**T** is for *tahimik*.
"*Shh* ... **quiet**!" Mama says to me
while praying in church
or reading in the library.

**U** is for *umaga*,
the end of the night—
when Mama kisses me good **morning**, and
dark becomes light.

**V** is for *Vigan*,
an **old northern town**
with Spanish-style mansions
and beautiful furniture renowned.

26

**W** is for *wala*,
meaning "absent" or "**none**."
When I wanted a cookie,
Yaya said, "*Wala*, not even one."

X-RAY
ROOM
A

▲ X-RAY ROOM A
◄ X-RAY ROOM B
EXAM ROOM I ►

**X** is for **X-ray**,
just like in English we say.
But in proper Tagalog
it's written *eksrey*.

**Y** is for *Yaya*,
my **nanny**, so sweet.
She loves me like a mother,
with a tenderness so complete.

29

**Z** is for **zipper**,
a word we hear every day.
But in Tagalog
it's *siper* we say.

# List of Words

**A**nak    Son

**B**utiki    Lizard

**C**hamporado
Chocolate-and-rice porridge

**D**ahon    Leaves

**E**wan    'Don't know'

**F**ilipino    Person born in
the Philippines

**G**aling    Praise

**H**ati    Divide

**I**bon    Bird

**J**eepneys    Buses

**K**umot    Blanket

**L**ola    Grandmother

**M**edyas    Stockings

**N**aku    'Oh no!'

**O**spital    Hospital

**P**ansit    Noodles

**Q**uezon    Manuel L. Quezon

**R**elo    Timepiece

**S**alamat    Thank you

**T**ahimik    Quiet

**U**maga    Morning

**V**igan    Historic town

**W**ala    None

**X**-ray    (Eksrey)

**Y**aya    Nanny

**Z**ipper    (Siper)